Know Your Numbers

Eggs and Legs

Counting in Twos

by Michael Dahl
illustrated by Todd Ouren

Raintree is an imprint of Capstone Global Library Limited,
a company incorporated in England and Wales having its
registered office at 264 Banbury Road, Oxford, OX2 7DY –
Registered company number: 6695582

www.raintree.co.uk
myorders@raintree.co.uk

Text © Capstone Global Library Limited 2020
The moral rights of the proprietor have been asserted.

Edited by Catherine Neitge and Christianne Jones
Designed by Todd Ouren
Original illustrations © Capstone Global Library Limited 2020
Production by Laura Manthe
Originated by Capstone Global Library Limited
Printed and bound in India

ISBN 978 1 4747 9119 9 (hardback)
ISBN 978 1 4747 9125 0 (paperback)

British Library Cataloguing in Publication Data
A full catalogue record for this book is available from the
British Library

Acknowledgements
We would like to thank Stuart Farm, M.A., Mathematics
Lecturer at the University of North Dakota, USA, and Susan
Kesselring, M.A., Literacy Educator, for their invaluable help in
the preparation of this book.

Mrs Hen stared at her empty nest.

TWO little legs went
running into the barn.

FOUR little legs were hiding in the corn.

2 4

7

SIX little legs were chasing the dog.

8

EIGHT little legs were jumping on a cow.

2 4 6 8

11

12

TEN little legs were climbing on the tractor.

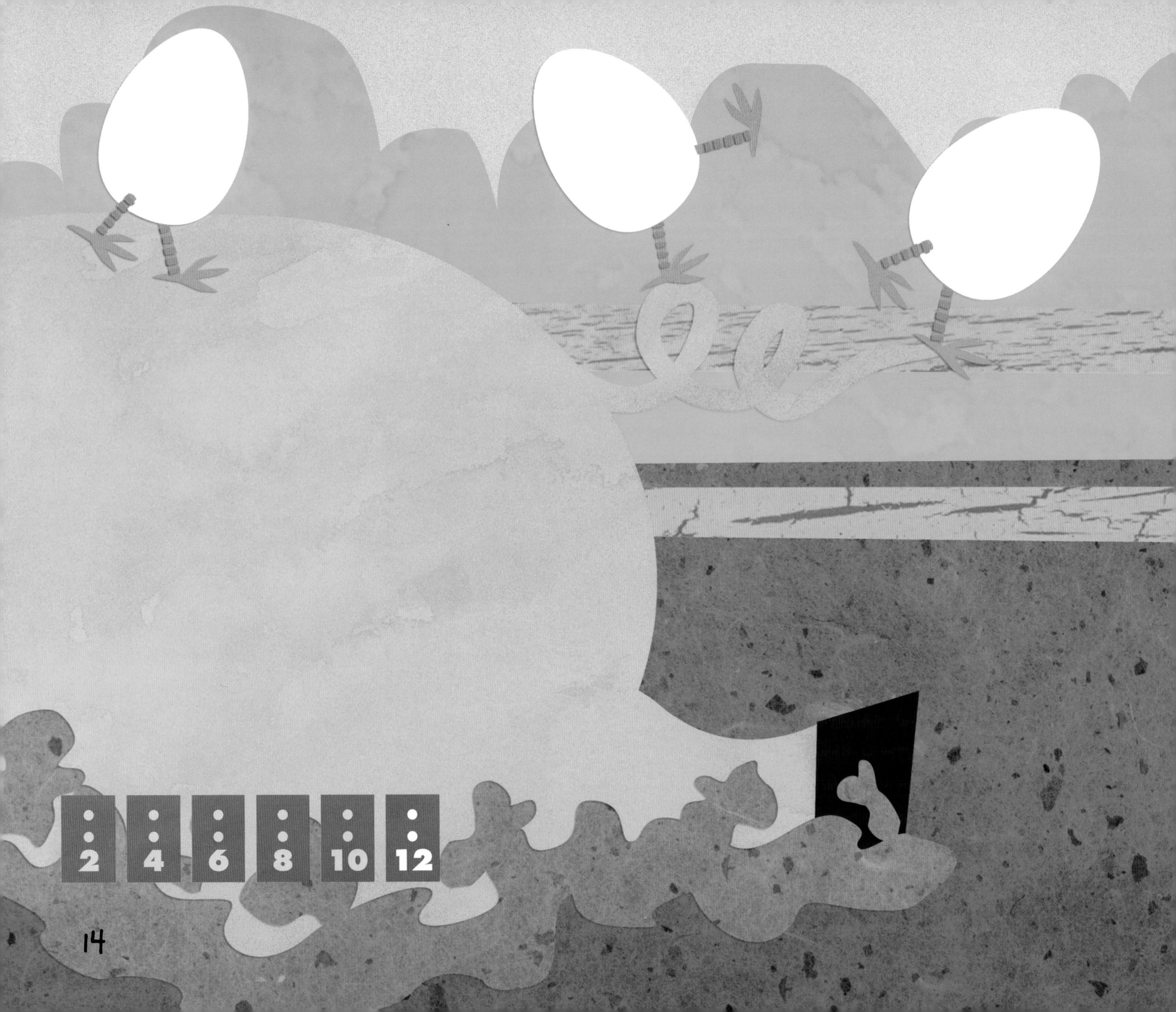
2
4
6
8
10
12

TWELVE little legs were playing with the pig.

FOURTEEN little legs were scurrying through the beans.

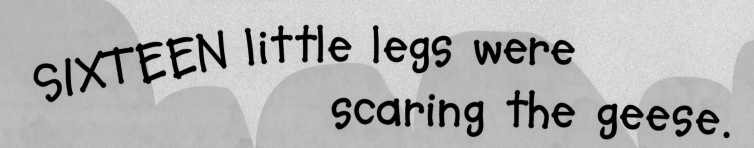

SIXTEEN little legs were
scaring the geese.

2 4 6 8 10 12 14 16

18

19

EIGHTEEN little legs were scooped up by the farmer's wife.

TWENTY little legs
were back in the nest.

2 4 6 8 10 12 14 16 18 20

22

"Phew!" said Mrs Hen. "These chicks really keep me on my toes!"

Fun facts

- A hen lays an average of 300 eggs a year.

- A mother hen turns over her eggs about 50 times a day.

- The heaviest ever chicken egg weighed just over 450 grams (16 ounces).

- Most chicken eggs are either white or brown, but some chickens lay blue-green eggs.

- There are more chickens in the world than people.

- The record number of yolks found in an egg is 9.

Find the numbers

Now you have finished reading the story, but a surprise still awaits you. Hidden in each picture is a multiple of 2 from 2 to 20. Can you find them all?

2 — the hook above the door
4 — the handle of the shovel
6 — on the wheelbarrow wheel
8 — the pulley on the well
10 — on the tractor engine
12 — on the mud splash on the right page
14 — above the beans on the right page
16 — between the wings of the goose
18 — between the four eggs on the left
20 — on the bottom right eggshell